DESTINED

for

GRACE

DESTINED FOR GRACE
Marty Delmon

Published by:
RPJ & COMPANY, INC.
P.O. Box 160243 | Altamonte Springs, FL 32716-0243 | 407.551.0734
www.rpjandco.com

ISBN-13: 978-0-9828277-0-3
ISBN-10: 0-98282770-9

Cover Image:
Never Alone © James Steidl - Fotolia.com

Cover & Interior Design:
Kathleen Schubitz
RPJ & COMPANY, INC.
www.rpjandco.com

Scripture quote on cover: 2 Peter 3:18, KJV

Scripture taken from the New King James Version, unless otherwise noted. Copyright © 1982 by Thomas Nelson, Inc. Used by permission. All rights reserved.

Printed in the United States of America.

DESTINED

for

GRACE

MARTY DELMON

RPJ & Company, Inc.
www.rpjandco.com

Table of Contents

PREFACE

Have you read my testimony? Well, buckle yourself in, I'm having another go at it. This time it will really be worth your while. This time I'll pull out the nuggets! But first let me flatten the earth.

A reader indicated she thought me rather low to write about my husband's homosexuality. Much of my story is wrapped up in my ex-husband's prior homosexuality. I say 'prior homosexuality' because today he lives without it. He's delivered. He's free. But since I wanted to write about his battle, before I started writing *Sleeping With Demons*, my first book, I asked his permission to put it into print.

He agreed. Why would he do such a public and humiliating thing? Because he, like any other servant of God, wants to do whatever it takes to bring people to Christ and to help them be free. He wrote a letter saying I had his permission to use his story however I saw fit. Therefore, I try to tell it exactly as I experienced it without adding frills or dark innuendoes. His story stands on its own; I don't need to fabricate anything.

Of course the best part is that he is whole now and serves the Lord with all his heart. He's part of the staff at the Christian facility that got him set free. Apparently he has great success in helping others get free as multitudes of men are grateful for his labor on their behalf. I am proud of him.

Every year we get together as a family for Christmas and from time to time during the year we send cornball emails to each other. When we're together we chat like an old hen and an old rooster. We are friends. He's serving the Lord in the States and I'm serving the Lord in France. What better thing could be said of our lives?

I also want to mention a remark made about my *Destined for Healing* book. A reader commented about being honored to know me because of the gifting that is in me. Please, don't be honored to know me or the gifting that is in me. Be honored to know the Giver of the gifts. The closest I come to claiming fame on terra firma is being the mother of the two greatest kids God ever sent to this earth. The Bible says gifts are given to those who desire them. That's all it takes to have a gift from God. Desire is also all it takes to have extraordinary experiences with the Lord.

He wants you, above all else, to know Him. He's like any other lover. He doesn't want shallow love. You wouldn't want that from your loved ones either. Don't just love the surface; get to know the depth. Talk to Him. Do things with Him. Go places with Him. Desire costs little or nothing; it just takes time.

Those of you who already know this have greater experiences than I do. I write these books for myself as well as you, to encourage you and me to reach for more. The depth, the height, the width, the length -- you'll never arrive at the end of God, so keep on pressing into Him, the Lover of your soul!

Grace Came

One Christmas season my children were in bed and my husband sat on the couch while I lit all the candles in the living room, at least two dozen. Then I stood back to admire my handiwork. I felt elegant that night. My husband tended to buy me articles of clothing made for someone with very small hips, not mine, but that night the slim line green velvet robe fit perfectly. To tell the truth, I felt attractive.

In this heady self-appraisal, I stood in front of him and asked a question I had asked dozens of times: "What is wrong with our marriage?" I just couldn't put my finger on it. Whatever was wrong was no doubt my fault, but how can you fix something if you don't know what it is?

For years afterward he told me that was one question he wished he'd never answered. He mildly said, "I like boys."

The gentle Christmas carols playing in the background wouldn't carry me to an understanding of what he had said, "What?" I asked.

"I prefer men."

I still didn't get it. "What does that mean?"

Rather pointedly he said, "I like making love with other men."

I had no more questions. I sat down hard on the edge of the couch beside him, my face no doubt etched in an extreme expression of shock. I must have collapsed as the next thing I knew he was kneeling over me, his hands pinning my shoulders to the floor. "Don't hate me! Don't hate me!"

Hate? That didn't register. He had just taken an emotional baseball bat and hit me squarely in the gut. I could barely breathe. What was he talking about? I should be the one yelling that at him. I felt hated, despised, ashamed, used, deceived, abused and a multitude of other emotions all roiling around inside of me.

"Who do you make love to?"

He told me. I knew the one he loved. He'd been faithful to one lover since several years before our wedding. They worked together so they were with each other every workday and had sex as often. Now I knew what was wrong with our marriage.

That's the last time I was able to fit into that green robe. We stayed together. Why? I wasn't certain after awhile, but I think it was for the kids. I'm sure it was. However, my depression spread like blood from a gunshot wound. I couldn't contain it.

Finally, I did practically nothing. I sat in my rocking chair and rocked and cried. I thought suicidal thoughts and then my children would come home from school, throw themselves in my arms, cuddling up on the chair with me, and I knew I couldn't do it. They knew they were saving me too, as they wiped the tears from my cheeks.

Some long-forgotten friends from halfway across the country happened to call at this time, wanting to know if they could visit. They arrived carrying home sales products in several suitcases and before they left I had signed up for their multi-level-marketing company and bought everything they had brought. Was I eager to get into business? Did I want that stuff? No. I was too depressed to refuse.

When they left I tried to think of someone I could sell these things to and thought of an aunt up in the foothills of California. I needed a weekend away so I left the kids with friends and drove up to see her. She didn't seem to notice my lack of energy. When I asked if she'd sign up for this company and buy some products, she said, "Sure, but I've got a prayer meeting to go to. Come with me and we'll talk about it afterward."

One of her boyfriends picked us up in his pickup truck and off we went, me in the middle, my head lying back on the seat, staring at the ceiling. My aunt needed the window for her cigarette smoke. I could tell the boyfriend thought I was really weird, but I didn't care.

Being an abnormally hot night in northern California, and since mountain churches don't have air conditioning, the little group pulled chairs into the parking lot. There were probably twelve in the circle. The Pastor explained the protocol of the prayer meeting and as he spoke I reflected. I'd never done anything like that before. Sure, I'd thrown prayers up to heaven like anyone else, but I never waited for a reply. I never expected a reply. But this night I noticed something new in me. I was willing.

When everyone closed their eyes, I did too. In front of me I saw a bright, white ball of light floating in the middle of the circle, larger than a man could stand in. A wind emanated from the ball, a wind so strong I felt my hair being whipped back tight against my head. A heat came pouring from the light making me think my skin would peel off from the burning.

My logical mind had to explain this phenomenon so I said to myself, 'A wind has come up and the sun is setting and is on you full force.' So I opened one eye to check it out. There wasn't even a breeze in the trees and the sun had already set. So I closed my eye again.

The phenomenon remained. I knew I had a choice. I could open my eyes and sit there while everyone else prayed, or I could get up and leave the premises, or I could watch this light and see what would happen. I wanted to watch and see. So I did.

Suddenly Jesus stepped out of the light. He looked like all the Sunday School pictures I'd seen of Him, mild, light brown hair, shoulder length, thin, wearing a white robe tied at the waist with a white rope. But His eyes I'd never seen before. They were like pale blue diamonds with intense flares of light flashing off their facets and when He looked at me I could not disengage my gaze from His. The light from His eyes seemed to scour the inside of my body, leaving it almost hollow.

He held out His arms and said, "Come to Me." It was so real I started to get out of my chair when the Pastor said, "Amen." As suddenly as that light appeared when I closed my eyes, it vanished as I opened my eyes. I looked around wondering why everyone was standing up. We'd only been there a few minutes. Was that all the praying we were going to do?

I looked at my watch. 10 minutes past 10 p.m. We'd been praying for over two hours! I had been entranced with Jesus for two hours! What had happened to me? I didn't know and I wasn't about to tell anybody. I didn't want people to think I was crazy.

We drove home, me in the middle again, with my aunt and her boyfriend talking over me. They seemed to be arguing over what had happened at the prayer meeting, but I was concerned with something entirely different. The ball of light may have disappeared when I opened my eyes, but something about that ball came home with me and rode in that truck!

It never left me. It went back to San Francisco with me. It spoke to me in a very soothing voice and said things to me on the inside of my chest, or from around my head, or so it seemed. Nice things. Things that made me feel better about myself. The depression lessened. The suicide thoughts no longer threatened. I even started going to church.

I chose the church because a famous architect designed it; they had a children's choir with the cutest robes so my children could sing and look adorable; and it was within walking distance of my home. All of that was well and good, except that every time I entered the door to the Sanctuary I started crying and I could not for the life of me figure out why.

Embarrassed, I sat in the back pew under an eave where nobody else sat so that my condition would not be noticed. People that I considered to be real misfits attended this church and never would I allow them to see me in such a pitiful condition! So there I sat, Sunday after Sunday, hiding, condescending, destroyed.

One Sunday, while walking to church, I heard an audible voice speak. It came from in front of me and just over my head. The idea of even hearing a non-existent, audible voice caused me to simply react. It spoke; I responded.

"Marty, you've come a long way, but you have one more step to take."

"What?"

"You must say with your mouth that I am your Lord."

Rage rose on the inside of me, right there on the sidewalk. No one was going to be my lord but me! At church I put the kids in the choir and headed for the door to the Sanctuary, only this time when I opened it, no tears came. I threw myself into that pew under the eave and steamed with fury. But something very calm inside of me let me know that if I said no to this audible voice, I would lose the soothing presence that had been making me feel better and better.

This church was of the Anglican variety and at the appointed time the congregation went forward by pews, knelt at the altar and took communion. As timing would have it, I had the altar rail to myself for a few seconds before others arrived and knelt beside me. In that core moment I looked at the empty cross and said, "Okay, Jesus. You are my Lord."

In one fell motion, like a tiny tempest, something cold and nasty left my body through the bottom of my feet, chased away by something warm and wonderful entering my body through my head and chest. It filled me. Completely. I didn't notice I had been served the bread and had eaten it.

At the precise moment I felt this infilling topping me up, a layman stood before me with the cup of wine.

"Marty, the blood of Jesus shed for you." I took the chalice and drank.

I must have gone back to my pew. The service must have ended. I must have collected my kids from Sunday School. I don't remember. I've had surgeries where the post-op was kind of like that. I must have been wheeled to a recovery room. I must have woken up. I must have wanted water, or a pain pill, or food. I don't remember. I just remember waking up in my hospital room hours later.

Suddenly I 'came to' in the brick courtyard of the church. I had a cup of coffee in my hand. My kids were playing tag with others nearby. Never had we stopped for the coffee hour after church. I looked over the crowd. *Omigosh! There's Betty and Gordy! How great to see them again! Wonder what they're up to?*

This couple had been some of the people in the church whom I had identified as 'misfits' just 45 minutes earlier. The layman who served the wine approached me. "Is your name Marty?"

I nodded my head. *Isn't that what he called me at the altar?* He looked so relieved I wanted to pat his arm to reassure him. "The Lord told me to say, 'Marty, the blood of Jesus shed for you.' and I argued with Him. I said, 'Lord, Marty is a man's name. If I say that she'll be offended.' But He insisted, so I said it."

"That's good," I said. "Because I had just finished telling Him He is my Lord."

The man's eyes widened. "You mean to tell me you got born again at the altar when I served you the wine?"

I shrugged. *What on earth is this guy talking about?* I smiled as he introduced me to his wife, genuinely glad to meet these people and happy to accept her invitation to lunch the following week. She also invited Betty and some other 'outcasts' who became close friends. I don't think I stopped smiling for about two and a half years. Everything went my way. Even when I didn't know what way I wanted things to go, they went my way.

We moved to the suburbs shortly after my 'new birth', so I set about the task of finding a house. I visited every house for sale in the area in which we wanted to move and nothing impressed me. Every time I scouted the area, I drove up a certain cul de sac where a house was for sale and every time I drove right back out without stopping. The house was too ugly. There was absolutely no curb appeal.

One day, after another fruitless hunt and under the pressure of getting my children settled before school started, I prayed. "Okay, Lord, the time has come; I need to find a house." That night I had a dream. I dreamed about a house whose living room, dining room, kitchen, family room, office and master bedroom were all upstairs and three children's bedrooms and a playroom were downstairs. When I woke up I screwed up my face, *Who would want a house like that? It's upside-down!*

My husband, tired of no results, told me to make some appointments and after work he wanted to see some of the houses I had rejected. The only house that would give us an appointment was the one on the cul de sac that I had never seen.

The front door was actually double doors and the woman opened them both, standing back to give us a full view into the house. A floor to ceiling stone fireplace faced the two doors about twenty feet away. Angling off to the right the living room faced the hearth. Angling off to the left the dining room enjoyed the fireplace. On the other side, the hearth being open on both sides, the family room/kitchen benefitted from the fire as well.

There were so many plate glass windows I wondered where the pillars were that held the house up. Outside the plate glass windows in the family room/kitchen a 500 year old oak grew through a hole in the middle of the decking. Those redwood boards stretched out from the house with as much square footage as the interior and they covered the slope of a hillside. Over the railing around the deck the swimming pool could be seen on the lower level. The children's bedrooms opened onto the pool. Everything just as in my dream.

I loved the house. I wanted to put an offer on it right then and there, but the owner told me I was too late.

Someone had put in a bid and would take ownership the next week. Confused, I wondered: *Lord, why would You have me dream about a house I can't have?* However, the next week the couple who had put in the bid dropped out; apparently they could not obtain the financing. God knew that. He knows the future, but I don't. We quickly bought the house before someone else could get a bid in.

This is just an example of how those first two and a half years of my Christian life unfolded. Everything was rosy. My husband even gave up his lover. I was happy! I said of myself, *I'm in seventh heaven!*

What happened to me that made me go from absolute despondency to absolute happiness? Grace came. The minute I closed my eyes in that prayer meeting, the Holy Spirit of God met me and never left me alone after that. He rearranged my thinking and gave me a new heart; He ordered my footsteps and made sure I received what heaven had sent. When Jesus Christ became my Lord, He deposited God's gift of grace in me. Grace, glorious grace.

There were trials during this time. Satan tries very hard to get a new born Christian to abandon Jesus. It's easier for Satan to trip Christians up and cause new-borns to give up when there is no foundation. That's what the enemy of God banks on. Taking the parable of the seed being sown, it might indicate that 25% of those born again will leave Jesus because they have no spiritual foundation. The seed falls by the wayside and birds come and eat the seed.

Thank God for a Christian culture. Those of us in the United States at least have our culture, which up until now has directed us to Christianity and given us knowledge of Jesus and His sacrifice for us. Another 25% will fall away because the seed fell on stony places with not much earth to sustain it. Fortunately for me a hunger to read the Bible overtook me and the root of the seed grew big and strong!

Another 25% will wither because of the thorns which are the cares of this world or the chasing after riches. Both of these have overwhelmed me from time to time, but thank God for grace which demonstrated the brilliance of letting God handle the cares of this world, of allowing Him to provide the riches.

One of the riches He provided was my dream house, so let's get back to that. To buy my dream house we had to sell the building in which we lived in San Francisco. Situated right in the heart of Cow Hollow, the lower border of Pacific Heights, this prime location property had three flats, each about 2,000 sq ft. A developer drooled over the possibility of making the three flats into three condos and selling each one for the original purchase price.

We thought about doing the remodeling ourselves, but we also needed the money from the sale of the building to finish paying for our portion of four restaurants. So we accepted his offer and to put it frankly, the developer swindled us. He gave us enough money to make a down payment on our house, promising us the bulk of our price later. What happened next I think came because he realized he didn't have the resources to pull off the real estate coup he'd hoped to have.

He told us he wasn't paying us the rest of the money. My husband arranged a meeting with him and I stayed home and prayed. I didn't know much about prayer at that time. I only knew how to talk to the Presence that had been with me since that prayer meeting in the foothills.

In those days giving my body something to do while I prayed helped a lot, so I went down and cleaned the pool. I took the long pole with the brush on the end and slid it down the sides of the pool, dislodging the growth that puffed out like a little cloud of rust as I swept.

I noticed an anger in me, an anger which I did not express. It's as if it wasn't mine. With every stroke I discussed different aspects of the situation with the Lord, talking it out, and that anger seemed to expand, still separate from me, however.

My husband arrived home about the time I finished the pool. Laying the pole in its usual resting place in a bed of ivy, I went up to the kitchen. My husband was not happy. The developer had offered to give us two little pieces of property as an advance on what he owed us. An inadequate band-aid on the wound, as it were.

I stood at the kitchen center island, leaning on the cooktop, looking at my husband standing by the sink. I said, "Why would God do this to us right when our son is headed for the University of California? We won't have the money to send him."

Suddenly I saw the truth and I wheeled around to declare that truth to the air in the family room. I shouted, "God is not doing this! It's you, Satan! Let me tell you this: In the name of Jesus Christ of Nazareth, my son will have all the education he wants and it will be paid for. We have no worries about money. God supplies it all. Therefore, Satan, you get your filthy, stinking hands off our money!"

I didn't have the good sense to know how to say that. I was a baby Christian. No one had taught me the ways of the Lord. I didn't know my authority. I didn't know grace, even though I was living in it. Where did those words come from? It was the Holy Anger of the Lord speaking through me by the Holy Spirit. It had been building up in my spirit, as that's where the Holy Spirit lives, and at the appointed time it erupted out of my mouth.

Here's the result of my proclamation: the developer gave us three buildings. The third one he added was his own home, a fabulous three story house in exclusive Marin County whose decked roof had a hot tub and a full view of the whole bay area. He and his wife intended to move to Spain. We sold the three and came up shy of our price by $50,000. The full story of that $50,000 is in my *Destined for Success* book.

As for my son, he went to the University of California for several years but graduated from Oral Roberts University. Then he received a diploma from Rhema Bible School. After that he graduated from Denver University Law School. He passed the California Bar Exam to qualify to practice law in the States, but he kept going. He got an international law degree from the University of Paris Deux, Pantheon-Sorbonne and passed tests that allow him to practice law in France. Then he passed his Bar Exam in England and Wales and recently obtained his PhD in Law from King's College at the University of London. He told me he finally has all the education he wants. And yes, it was all paid for, by grace.

> *For you know the grace of our Lord Jesus Christ, that though He was rich, yet for your sakes He became poor, that you through His poverty might become rich (2 Corinthians 8:9).*

Perhaps you're like me; I need for things to be spelled out. I need to know exactly what grace is. So, let me explain.

Grace Explained

From the time I was born again in 1979, I have read the Bible through from cover to cover every year. The Word is the only thing that feeds our spirits and I have learned to enjoy that food! Thirty one years later, I still read through it every year. I try not to read it with my mind; in fact, I try to train myself to pray in tongues while I read it. Notice I use the word 'try.' It has yet to become a habit. You may ask why I bother. Because so much more is revealed that way! One thing is for sure: with this finite mind I will never comprehend all the millions of layers of revelation hidden in the Word. Of all the words therein, 'grace' has the most revelatory layers that I have found in the Bible, so far.

Grace is such a big word in the New Testament that Paul, recognized as the writer of 14 letters, or books, opens 13 of them with the word 'grace' and ends all 14 with the word 'grace'. Yet, in my Bible study, I have found no discourse on what grace is. I can find explanatory teaching in the Word for just about every other subject, but not grace. That is rather disconcerting when one sets out to learn about a thing.

With some subjects God hides the meaning for those who will dig for it. There are nuggets hidden for the serious student, the profound lover of Jesus Christ. If He gave His gifts of truth that can be used for personal blessing to just anybody, then the world would become New Agers and seek to satisfy their own lusts. Instead, His grace is reserved only for His children, to be blessed and to be able to bless others.

The young preacher in Ephesus, Timothy, received two instructive letters from Paul that were included in the New Testament. In them Paul describes grace like this:

> **And the grace of our Lord was exceedingly abundant, with faith and love which are in Christ Jesus (1 Timothy 1:14).**

You can see from this Scripture that grace has two elements: Faith and Love. As I pointed out in my *Destined for Faith* book, faith also has two elements: Trust and Obedience. And as my book *Destined for Love* demonstrates, love has two elements: Surrender and Sacrifice.

In other words, what makes grace operate is faith and love. Likewise, what makes faith operate is trust and obedience and what makes love operate is surrender and sacrifice. In my mind's eye I see a very busy four lane highway flowing between me and God. My two lanes going to Him are loaded with faith and love. His two lanes coming to me are loaded with faith and love. It is a two way street. He needs my faith and love in order to operate His grace. He needs His faith and love in order to give me His grace.

Remember the man in the circus who walked on stilts? He could never stand still, could he? If he did put his legs together in a stationary pose, he would fall. His performance depended on his stilts being in constant motion. That's how God's grace is. Your stilts are named Faith and Love and you must keep your faith and love in constant motion in order to keep grace in operation.

That's why, in my early years of being a Christian, everything went my way. I was so in love with Jesus and trusted Him so completely that I never thought about anything else. Grace had full freedom in my life to give me full favor.

Another word about grace from Paul to Timothy goes as follows:

> **Who has saved us and called us with a holy calling, not according to our works, but according to His own purpose and grace which was given to us in Christ Jesus before time began (2 Timothy 1:9).**

This second Scripture explains that grace was given to you before time began. How? In Christ Jesus. That's a startling revelation to me. I knew God had a purpose for my life before He created the earth, but that He gave me grace, when I didn't even know what it was, that blew my mind! It took me long enough to accept my purpose! Here I am in my latter years and I'm just now stepping into the stride of fulfilling that purpose. And now I'm comprehending grace, a state of being which belongs only to those born of God.

The Israelites didn't have the grace of God. Grace was designated for surrendered believers in Christ. Jesus brought it. That dispensation was determined before time began. The Jews operated by their own works. True believers operate by His purpose and through His grace. Jesus gave you grace. Just like people give gifts to new babies, God sent grace with Jesus as His gift to you to celebrate your new birth. Grace is yours.

Notice what Paul told Timothy to do about grace:

> *You therefore, my son, be strong in the grace that is in Christ Jesus (2 Timothy 2:1).*

This third Scripture points out in no uncertain terms that grace needs you to be strong. In fact, it commands you to be strong, "You...be strong!" Strong in what? Strong in grace. How can you be strong in grace when you are not the one who makes it happen? You can be strong in faith and strong in love.

No one can make you strong but you. Physical strength is an example of that. Eating right and exercising will take you to the point of strength you desire. Nobody can do that for you. And God won't do it for you. Faith and love will take you to the point of strength in grace that you desire. Your level of strength depends on you.

When the subject of grace became so prominent in my reading, I began my quest to understand this grace I had been given. I started searching the Word beginning with John, my favorite book in the Bible.

> *And the Word became flesh and dwelt among us, and we beheld His glory, the glory as of the only begotten of the Father, full of grace and truth (John 1:14).*

> *And of His fullness we have all received, and grace for grace (V 16).*

> *For the law was given through Moses, but grace and truth came through Jesus Christ (V 17).*

The word 'grace' has been used culturally to indicate an outward expression. Grace in polite society means to have good manners, polite speech, accepting compliments and rebuff equally with aplomb, having straight posture, elegance in body movements, and so on. Today's society may not put as much emphasis on 'grace' as previous generations, but in general, social adroitness is what it means. Grace makes social interaction pleasant, which makes grace a rather lightweight subject.

However, these Scriptures in John equate grace with truth. Truth is a heavyweight subject! It's God's truth that rules and reigns. His truth makes you free. His truth is His Word. Jesus our Lord is His Word and therefore His truth.

Grace is equal to that! Therefore the above social description has nothing to do with God's massive grace. So what is it?

All my life I've heard that grace is unmerited favor. I used to think that was sweet. Oh, God does favors for me even when I don't deserve it. Isn't that precious? Now that I know more about grace I see that 'unmerited favor' is the weakest of weak definitions possible and I won't even use that description in my vocabulary.

The word "unmerited" puts the focus on me. Did I earn or not earn my new birth? Neither. I simply received it. Can I deserve or not deserve grace? Of course not! From the foundations of the earth God intended the gift of grace for me. So why put me in the equation at all? I don't belong there. Let's keep the word "favor", and I'll show you in a minute what to replace the word "unmerited" with.

There is also an acronym which goes like this: God's Riches At Christ's Expense. That comes closer but still does not describe grace in the fullness of what it is. It's basically another attempt by man to place grace in a box.

John also points out that grace is a new covenant gift and was not a part of the old covenant. Very little is found in the Old Testament about grace, other than people looked for grace and were happy when they found it. People looked for grace in the eyes of their king, or their master, or some other person in power. The references to God giving grace in the Old Testament spoke of the future. Peter lets his readers know that the Israelites wanted this grace, but didn't have it.

> *Of this salvation the prophets have inquired and searched carefully, who prophesied of the grace that would come to you (1 Peter 1:10).*

Luke equated great grace with great power.

> *And with great power the apostles gave witness to the resurrection of the Lord Jesus. And great grace was upon them all (Acts 4:33).*

On one of his journeys, Paul met with the elders in Ephesus and he told them the grace of God is the gospel, the good news. I always thought the death, burial and the resurrection of Jesus was the good news and it certainly is, but Paul says the gospel, the good news, is the grace of God. It's grace that took Jesus through that death, burial and resurrection. Just like it's grace that takes you through the difficult passages in your life. It's your good news! Jesus gave you the grace of God!

> *But none of these things move me; nor do I count my life dear to myself, so that I may finish my race with joy, and the ministry which I received from the Lord Jesus, to testify to the gospel of the grace of God (Acts 20:24).*

Twenty verses in the book of Romans speak about grace. I promise; I won't quote all twenty! But let's look at some of them.

> *Through whom also we have access by faith into this grace in which we stand, and rejoice in hope of the glory of God (Romans 5:2).*

> *But the free gift is not like the offense. For if by the one man's offense many died, much more the grace of God and the gift by the grace of the one Man, Jesus Christ, abounded to many (V 15).*

> *For if by the one man's offense death reigned through the one, much more those who receive abundance of grace, and of the gift of righteousness, will reign in life through the One, Jesus Christ (V 17).*

> *Moreover the law entered that the offense might abound. But where sin abounded, grace abounded much more (V 20).*

> *So that as sin reigned in death, even so grace might reign through righteousness to eternal life through Jesus Christ our Lord (V 21).*

At your new birth you received an abundance of grace, the grace of God, the unmerited favor people speak of.

You received everything that God could possibly give. 'Unmerited favor' doesn't begin to describe all that God gave you. Think of it! Through grace you are able to 'reign in life.' It takes abundant favor for that! He waited for this moment to give grace because it can only be given after you receive the gift of righteousness which comes from the death, burial and resurrection of Jesus Christ.

Part of your good news, part of the gospel you believe is that at your new birth you were given the ability to reign in life. You may wail, *'But I'm not! If anything, life is raining on me!'* I didn't say you are reigning, I said you were given the ability to reign. What you do with it is up to you. Let's look at Paul's exhortation to the Corinthians.

> *I thank my God always concerning you for the grace of God which was given to you by Christ Jesus (1 Corinthians 1:4).*

> *According to the grace of God which was given to me, as a wise master builder I have laid the foundation, and another builds on it. But let each one take heed how he builds on it (1 Corinthians 3:10).*

> *But by the grace of God I am what I am, and His grace toward me was not in vain; but I labored more abundantly than they all, yet not I, but the grace of God which was with me (1 Corinthians 15:10).*

> *For our boasting is this: the testimony of our*
> *conscience that we conducted ourselves in*
> *the world in simplicity and godly sincerity,*
> *not with fleshly wisdom but by the grace of*
> *God, and more abundantly toward you (2*
> *Corinthians 1:12).*

Replace that word 'unmerited' with 'full' and call grace the 'full favor of God', because that is what it is. Jesus brought it into the world and I think it was too awesome for the translators and teachers of the Word to actually proclaim. The fact that God would carefully construct His society was beyond political thinking. That Jesus would shape His body by giving each person a specific grace to be and to do what God Almighty decreed for them before the foundation of the earth was beyond any political thinking.

Man has always wanted to be in control, which means there has to be somebody to control. But God is pointing out in these verses that through Jesus you have grace for your place and in that place and through that grace you reign in life. No other human being reigns over you. That means Christians live in a Theocracy where the Godhead is the chief and Christians are rulers underneath Him, rulers of our own lives. Grace has given you everything you need for such an existence.

Up until now, in this chapter, I've been leading you as if you were watching a fireworks display. One beauty at a time is shot into the air and the crowd ooohhs and aaahhs. But the grand finale is when all kinds of aerial bombs are launched and the sky is flooded with grandeur. Here's the grand finale of what the Bible has to say about grace.

Blessed be the God and Father of our Lord Jesus Christ, who has blessed us with every spiritual blessing in the heavenly places in Christ (Ephesians 1:3).

Just as He chose us in Him before the foundation of the world, that we should be holy and without blame before Him in love (V 4).

Having predestined us to adoption as sons by Jesus Christ to Himself, according to the good pleasure of His will (V 5).

To the praise of the glory of His grace, by which He made us accepted in the Beloved (V 6).

In Him we have redemption through His blood, the forgiveness of sins, according to the riches of His grace (V 7).

Which He made to abound toward us in all wisdom and prudence (V 8).

> *Having made known to us the mystery of His will, according to His good pleasure which He purposed in Himself (V 9).*
>
> *That in the dispensation of the fullness of the times He might gather together in one all things in Christ, both which are in heaven and which are on earth—in Him (V 10).*

Christians live in a third dimension of life, not in bios or physical life, not in psyche or soulish life, but in Zoë life. Jesus came to give you Zoë life. That's where you live, you who are born again. As you can see from the verses of Ephesians 1, you have it all because of the gift of grace from the Father and what Jesus did to bring you that grace.

In Grace are found the following:

He gave you every spiritual blessing.
He chose you.
He made you holy.
He made you to be without blame.
He predestined you to be His child.
You are accepted in the Beloved.
He redeemed you.
He forgave your sins.
He gave you wisdom.
He gave you prudence.
He made you know the mystery of His will.
He poured out His good pleasure on you.
He gathers you to Himself through Jesus Christ.

Jesus said to her, "I am the resurrection and the life (Zoë). He who believes in Me, though he may die, he shall live. And whoever lives and believes in Me shall never die..." (John 11:25-26a).

That is the only life that can be lived through Jesus Christ; He came to give you Zoë. No one else can have this life. Zoe life is super-ability, super-human, divine-life, divine-ability, forever.

Two dimension humans – living only through the soul and the body - cannot be sons of God. You must live through your spirit to be called a son of God because that is how God leads you. (Romans 8:14) Religion cannot make you super-human. It's not until the life of Christ steps into your life and takes over that you have Zoë. You have received the power of God, super-human-ability, Zoë, through Christ.

Therefore there is nothing about you that is common. You are the image of God. You are the likeness of God. You have the attributes of God. You have the characteristics of God. You have the mind of Christ. You have received the Holy Spirit. You are the temple of the Living God. He lives in you. The Kingdom of God is in you. You have it all! You've been blessed with all spiritual blessings. You've been chosen, predestined, called, sanctified, glorified and it's all done. You have heaven on earth.

If you were to die right now, go to heaven and say to God, 'Oh, good, I'm here. I made it.' He would say, 'You've always been here. You've had heaven from the moment you received Jesus as Lord. Christ has been in you. My Spirit has been in you. My Nature has been in you. My Presence has been in you. You have every blessing, every ability, and every power to rule and reign on the earth.'

Most Christians would probably look at God and say, "I have? Where's it been? I certainly didn't know I had all that. And I certainly didn't know I ruled and reigned in life. It felt to me that circumstances rolled right over me. There was nothing I could do to prevent those circumstances because I didn't know they were coming and if I could have ruled over the solutions I would have definitely chosen something else to happen instead of what did happen. Where was all that stuff when I needed it?"

The verses from Ephesians quoted above are all written in past tense. Translators couldn't handle so much power and authority so they added the word 'shall' which puts stuff in the future, but the past tense shows you already are blessed. It's finished. God has already done it all and given it to you. That's grace.

The word heaven means the abode of God. He has chosen you to be His everlasting habitation. You love Him because He loved you first. You accepted Him because He chose you first. He made you in His image so that He could make His home in you. From His home in you He draws all men to Himself through His Son, Christ Jesus.

And I heard a loud voice from heaven saying, "Behold, the tabernacle of God is with men, and He will dwell with them, and they shall be His people. God Himself will be with them and be their God" *(Revelation 21:3).*

Are you the people of God?

Are you the image of God?

Are you made in the likeness of God?

Is Christ in you?

Are you born again?

Do you have the Holy Spirit?

Do you have the mind of the Spirit?

Do you know all things? (If you answer yes to the questions above you have to answer yes to this one, too. 1 John 2:20)

Is the Kingdom of God in you?

Then you're no longer a common person, aimlessly wandering through life. You are a citizen of heaven living in GRACE, the full favor of God. You have it all.

That is amazing grace.

People add the word 'unmerited' to the word 'favor' because the old nature wants to work for it.

That's why, IF, after living for a while in full favor, and you slowly switch over to trying to earn your place in grace, you experience a falling away. That's when you stand still on your stilts and fall because your two legs of faith and love have stopped moving. Then, having fallen, when you hunt for grace, you find grace has gone into shadow.

Grace in Shadow

I can remember when it happened. Would I have described it back then as Grace Lifting? Or the Holy Ghost Leaving? Or some other dramatic moniker? No, I would have said, "I remembered."

In our family room a large, round poker table stood in the corner where two plate glass windows met. Reputed to have been regularly used by Mark Twain and Bret Harte, the poker table became like a museum piece for us, however, we covered it with Plexiglas and used it for family meals. One plate glass window slid open as a door to the deck. The other displayed a compelling panorama.

A stand of tall bamboo swayed along the edges of a creek running down the boundary of our property beyond our pool and behind those stood stately Eucalyptus trees also obliging the wind. Apparently a storm was whipping up and I sat at the table to watch it sweep in. Peace and quiet inside; turbulence outside. Normally I kept Christian television on in the background so I could check in now and then to hear what they were saying. The TV was off.

At five that morning I'd gotten up for two hours of prayer, after which I got the kids off to school. From eight to ten I read the Word; then I ran errands. Now I sat in serene silence. I should have been at a spiritual peak.

In the quiet, a little memory tiptoed in and lifted the corner of my mind as elegantly as if it were sitting down to cover its legs with my blanket. Of course, once allowed that privilege, it scooted in even further. I remembered something mean my husband had done to me before Jesus saved me and grace came, and before I knew it I was crying.

Unfortunately, awareness of the encompassing grace eluded me. For the two and a half years since Jesus had filled me up at that altar, my husband's actions hadn't bothered me one bit. They were his actions, not mine. He chose how he treated me and I wasn't responsible for his behavior. Grace had quickly clarified my thinking that the old saying, "Now look what you made me do," simply had no truth in it. Nobody makes anybody do anything. We all choose our actions.

Shortly after being born again I discovered in the Bible that my husband had a spiritual obligation to make love to me whenever I wanted it. I spoke with him and he agreed we would make love once a week. You might be saying, 'that's not very much for a married woman,' or 'why not every night, or at least twice a week.' After having lived for 16 years with it happening once every three months, I thought once a week to be a landslide!

When I look back on those years I have to laugh at the antics my husband put himself through in order to avoid having sex with me. But on this day when 'I remembered', all I could think about were the mean things he had said during those 16 years to avoid what he found to be so distasteful. Furthermore, since my discovery of that Bible passage, he hadn't really been putting himself to the task. I always had to initiate things.

But now I remembered and those memories consumed me. They hurt. Those memories sailed soundlessly back into my mind like benign boats on the bay, which they weren't. They were lies. The things that hurt about those memories were how awful I felt about myself.

Grace had washed away those memories and those lies. For two and a half years I had indulged myself in the unrestrained pleasure of how wonderful God finds me to be, which meant my mind exercised itself on how wonderful I find God to be. But on this day those benign boats blocked my relationship with my wonderful Lord and I brooded.

That was enough for one day. Satan is clever. Had he overwhelmed me with all the memories in his arsenal, I would have seen his plot and driven him out. Sometimes he does overplay his hand, but on this day he acted prudently. He saved other memories for other days.

I can hear you. You're saying, 'Come on, Marty. Don't try to tell us you had actually forgotten those things. That's impossible.' Well, I hadn't remembered them, isn't that like forgetting? Once Grace Came, I didn't think about things like that. For those two and a half years, having fallen madly in love with Jesus, I only thought about Him. Truly.

At night I went to sleep telling Him how wonderful He was and how much I loved Him. I woke up with love for Him on my mind, usually singing something to Him from my heart. Many times I fell asleep singing to Him and I'd wake up singing the same song, even the same phrase. During the day, oh I planned, I suppose, but only moderately, only enough to get everything done that needed doing. I thanked Him during my days. If some kind of patriotic Jesus flag could be flown, it would look like me. I loved Him. I loved Him. I loved Him. That's all that could be said for those two and a half years.

I've since learned that's all grace requires; love Him and trust Him.

> *... singing with grace in your hearts to the*
> *Lord (Colossians 3:16b).*

It seems to me the mere fact of singing requires an attitude of love. Even in opera when one virtuoso sings his or her anger to another it ends up being a shout. I might sing *about* Him without actively loving Him, but I can't sing *to* Him without actively loving Him. Let me take you back to a previous Scripture.

> **And the grace of our Lord was exceedingly**
> **abundant, with faith and love which are in**
> **Christ Jesus (1 Timothy 1:14).**

This makes grace abundant: faith and love. Faith believes vehemently that Jesus has done it all for you and you can rest on that truth. Faith is really your Sabbath. Love? You're made in the image of God. What is He made of? Love. What, therefore, are you made of? Love. Just as God's love is centered on you, your love is centered on Him.

During those two and a half years I trusted God implicitly. It didn't occur to me to doubt. I had questions, incomprehension, which He readily answered, but I didn't doubt. I followed Him like Mary's little lamb. And I loved Him.

But when one is engaged in rummaging around in old, sordid memories, there's not much time for faith and love. Yet that's what happens. Your mind, which did not get made new in the new birth transaction, wants its control back. It's stocked to the gills with memories that need sorting out and eliminating, or so your mind would have you think.

Plus there are the lies planted by Satan in your soul that have been leading your life for years, even decades. So now you've got your emotions, your mind, your memory all clamoring for supremacy and you're wondering where the grace of God went. It's waiting for you under the shadow of His wing. When you turn again toward Him with the same childlike trust and the same first crush love you had at the beginning, you'll find yourself smack dab in the middle of grace.

A woman I knew in San Francisco had arthritis in her hands so crippling she could barely hold her silverware to eat. One day when I dropped in for a visit I noticed her hands were youthful, soft and supple with no signs of the debilitation I had seen before. Of course I wanted to know what had happened.

She had heard a doctor speak on the subject of arthritis. He had just written a book/cookbook about how to get rid of the disease through diet. She bought the book, followed his instructions and I could plainly see the results before my eyes.

Maybe a year later she and her husband invited me for lunch. Her hands were crippled like claws and her husband spent our lunch time feeding her. I asked what happened to the diet, thinking maybe the results were only temporary, but she floored me with what she said.

"Well, it's so hard to stay on a diet. I mean, I'd go to lunch with my friends and I'd want to eat what they were eating, so little by little my hands got worse than before."

Astounded I asked, "Can't you go back on the diet?"

"I just can't bring myself to do it."

She described the regime; it was nothing more than wholesome food. Surely for the sake of being able to feed herself she could follow a few dietary rules, but no. Wanting to be like everyone else ruined her health.

That's how the Body of Christ is with grace. You know how glorious it is to be in the fullness of grace, but will you, as a child of God, put aside old memories and debilitating lies in order to live in grace? Apparently not. You seem to want to live like the world, indulging in pity parties, bemoaning your state of affairs.

> **When he came and had seen the grace of God, he was glad, and encouraged them all that with purpose of heart they should continue with the Lord (Acts 11:23).**

Take this example. The people in Antioch were living in the grace of God, according to Barnabas' report. Yet he had to encourage them to purpose in their hearts to continue with the Lord. If they were living in the utopia of grace why would they need encouragement to stay there? Here's the secret: they could only stay there if they purposed in their hearts to stay. If they declined the persistent invitation of memories and lies to rejoin them, they could continue with the Lord.

The next time Barnabas went to Antioch he was with Paul and here is what they had to do.

> **Now when the congregation had broken up, many of the Jews and devout proselytes followed Paul and Barnabas, who, speaking to them, persuaded them to continue in the grace of God (Acts 13:43).**

They had to persuade them to continue in the grace of God! What was their alternative? Squabbling about law and traditions? How to get things just right? Doesn't that sound like the same as entertaining bad memories and lies? Let those things go and follow Jesus. But human nature has to try to resolve issues on its own. Human nature would rather work for grace than to freely receive it.

Paul wrote to the Romans about this very matter.

> ***What shall we say then? Shall we continue in sin that grace may abound? (Romans 6:1).***

> ***For sin shall not have dominion over you, for you are not under law but under grace (V 14).***

> ***What then? Shall we sin because we are not under law but under grace? Certainly not! (V 15).***

It's a struggle. It's a choice. Wrestle your soul to the ground and say, "You will follow Jesus! You will fix your total attention on Him! You will love Him, you will approve of Him, you will follow Him and you will enjoy Him." Because if you don't, you won't live under grace. It will be there in the shadows, waiting for you, but you have to choose to go to grace and not expect grace to overtake you. Why won't it? Because it already did. You chose to go back to old memories, old lies and old behaviors.

Since Paul brings up the sticky subject of sin, let's look at that. The word 'sin' means to miss the mark. You have a conscience that can tell you exactly where the mark is that you don't want to miss and normally you aim exactly for that mark. Except that society, according to popularized bends in the road that vary in each new generation, determines that certain sins are not only desirable, but acceptable.

Let's take a current issue: illicit sex. There seems to be no such word as 'licit' but let's coin it anyway. 'Licit' sex would indicate sex within marriage between husband and wife. Anything outside of that would be sin. Today these limitations are practically nonexistent, especially among Baby Boomers, those who were born after Dad came home from World War II. The hapless result for those who throw away all restraint is that they find themselves living in a murky mental morass, even though society now condones illicit sex.

By government statistics in France, 85% of married couples will have multiple affairs. I have spoken with couples who told me how they counsel each other in their extramarital affairs and they openly do this because the practice is so overtly accepted. On the dark side of this behavior, France beats us hands down in taking anti-depressants. They are a somber people. Sad. No longer aiming for the mark causes them to live in darkness and grace has been pushed from their borders.

The beloved disciple, John, writes of this condition.

> *This is the message which we have heard from Him and declare to you, that God is light and in Him is no darkness at all (1 John 1:5).*

> *If we say that we have fellowship with Him, and walk in darkness, we lie and do not practice the truth (V 6).*

> *But if we walk in the light as He is in the light, we have fellowship with one another, and the blood of Jesus Christ His Son cleanses us from all sin (V 7).*

Now let's be clear about one thing. God is the mark. With all your mental processes, your decisions and all your behavior it is God you are aiming for, that is, if you choose to aim for the mark. Its His Word that lets you know that sex outside of marriage is not wise, to say the least. It's darkness.

Does that mean that God looks at the one participating in illicit sex abhorrently? No. He doesn't look at the darkness. He walks in the light. It's you who choose to walk in darkness and you who have to deal with the consequences. Society makes it extremely easy to walk in this darkness, so much so that the world no longer even considers illicit sex to be a sin.

However, if you choose, even in a state of sin, to look at the light, to walk with Him in His purity of holiness, you will be in fellowship with Him and you will be cleansed. After awhile the desire to sin will disappear and the blood of Jesus Christ His Son will cleanse you from all sin. As in all things, it is always a choice: put your attention on Him or put your attention on the sin.

Listen carefully to how John explains what he just wrote.

> *If we say that we have no sin, we deceive ourselves, and the truth is not in us (1 John 1:8).*

> *If we confess our sins, He is faithful and just to forgive us our sins and to cleanse us from all unrighteousness (V 9).*

> *If we say that we have not sinned, we make Him a liar, and His word is not in us (V 10).*

John is writing to believers and therefore he is writing to you. John admonishes you not to deceive yourself. You sin. Admit it; you do. Your skirts may be perfectly clean, but what about that thought life? Thoughts, words, deeds, in these three you sin. But God's not concerned as long as you walk with Him in His light, confess your fall and with your focus on Him the cleansing comes. Sin dies away. You've hit the mark.

But if you deliberately choose to sin, even justifying it not only to yourself but to others, and determine you are going to do this sin no matter what, you will walk in darkness and grace will not operate in your life. There is no need to outline the nasty consequences of intentional sin, you already know that state of being. You already know how your premeditated sin not only damages you, but also those attached to you, those you love. So don't lie to yourself. Aim for God. Live in His Grace.

Let's get back to Paul as he deals with the Romans along these lines.

> *I beseech you therefore, brethren, by the mercies of God, that you present your bodies a living sacrifice, holy, acceptable to God, which is your reasonable service (Romans 12:1).*

> *And do not be conformed to this world, but be transformed by the renewing of your mind, that you may prove what is that good and acceptable and perfect will of God (V 2).*

> *For I say, through the grace given to me, to everyone who is among you, not to think of himself more highly than he ought to think, but to think soberly, as God has dealt to each one a measure of faith (V 3).*

Your body has its own memories and lies to deal with. They say a dog will avoid the street corner where a car hit it. Once hurt, twice cautious. You know where I'm going with this. Something bad happens to you and you say, 'I'll never let THAT happen again.' And you build a defensive wall inside of yourself. Those decisions are like strongholds.

For instance, I have a friend who is perpetually late to meet me anywhere. She will be 30 to 45 minutes late every time. At first I lightly chided her and she brushed it off with comments about being from the south and that's just how southerners are. Then I told her plainly how much it bothered me and after that she always had good, strong excuses for why she was late. I told her there is no such thing as a good excuse, but she continues to make them.

In a flare of anger I decided I would be late for her. If we agreed to meet at noon, I knew she'd arrive at 12:30. So I arrived at 1:00. Now let me apprise you, I am on time, if not early, to every appointment I have. My friend right away accused me of paying her back and I shrugged and gave her a very good excuse why I was late.

This went on for a couple of months. The problem was I didn't like myself very much for doing this so I decided to be on time again and just bring a book whenever I was to meet her. However, I couldn't do it. I could be on time for everyone else, but not for this friend. Finally I realized I had made that decision in anger and that anger nailed the decision to the floor of my soul.

I had to take drastic action in the other direction in order to get rid of that decision. I had to confess to my friend and apologize. We've gone back to our old ways; she's late and I wait. Frankly, I'd like to give her up as a friend because of these kinds of patterns in her, but I can't bring myself to do it. As a child, blubbering over the disloyalty of my mom, I made a decision I would be loyal to a fault. That kind of loyalty quite often gets me in trouble.

Now let's look at all this in relationship to our Scripture from Romans 12:1-3. ***Present your bodies a living sacrifice....*** Being on time is a good thing. Making your bed in the morning is a good thing. Keeping your car clean is a good thing. But the perfect thing is to present your body to the Lord as a living sacrifice, in other words, doing what He wants you to do and not what you've determined is the right thing to do.

One time the Lord told me not to make my bed. This was not freedom for me. I'd walk by that bedroom door and cringe to see my bed unmade. Somewhere along the line I had decided that people who don't make their beds are unruly, undisciplined people and I wasn't about to be like that. I asked, "Lord, why do You want me not to make my bed?" He let me know it was to show me the power of my mind. I couldn't help myself. All day long I wandered by my bedroom door looking at my unmade bed and shuddering from the desire to make it. The power my mind had over me astounded me.

Since then I still make my bed, but if I happen to get up late for an appointment, I'll rush out of the house without making it. When I get home and see it unmade I might crawl back in for a nap. Then what's the point of making it when

I'll just be getting back into it in a few hours? In other words, my mind is no longer attached to the making of my bed.

Be transformed by the renewing of your mind.... Using your brain is a good thing. Having memories is a good thing. Transformation is a good thing. But the perfect thing is to think about what the Lord wants you to think about, in other words, letting the Holy Spirit speak to your mind so you can meditate on God's plans and not what you've determined to think about. The transformation will come when all the lies and emotions of memories have been levered out of your life from lack of attention. If you don't feed something it eventually dies. Don't feed those lies and memories!

If you say you're not going to think about a thing that's almost like insurance that you will think about it. It's a useless battle to say, 'No, I won't think about that. Nope. Not me. I won't think about that.' You'll find yourself *only* being able to 'think about that'. What does work is to engage your mind in thinking about something else.

If you think about the Lord's subjects, meditate on the Word of God for example, remember the last things He said to you personally, or analyze larger more global subjects, like grace, you'll have revelation and direction instead of spiraling down and groveling in self-pity and self-abuse. More importantly, you will have displaced those destructive thoughts.

I marvel that you are turning away so soon from Him who called you in the

grace of Christ, to a different gospel (Galatians 1:6).

Turning away to what? Your own efforts to rescue yourself? Your own taking care of your wounds? Your own nurturing of the cherished lies you believe? Trust me; I learned the hard way that this is what I was doing.

First I decided I needed deliverance. After all, I had heard sermons about it. Becoming more and more tormented by fears and hurts, I sought out the help of a renowned deliverance team, at least they were well known in our area. There were four of them on the team. We met in their church. At first, while I was telling them my story they all sat real close to me, chummy, encouraging me to tell every sordid detail.

When it came time for the deliverance they made me sit on the other side all alone and the four of them sat against the other wall. They told me they didn't want the demons jumping on them. They also told me that I would know if the demons left as with the exit of each one I would either cough or yawn.

For the next two hours I coughed and yawned all over the place while they commanded any demon they could think of that could be associated with my story to leave me. Finally I left them knowing that absolutely nothing had happened. Looking back I can see that these were spiritual children playing childish spiritual games. They meant well. They, however, were not being led by the Holy Spirit. I'm sure they were making up names for demons that don't even exist! They were determining how to rescue me, while I was determining the means by which I should be rescued. The blind leading the blind.

Then I decided I needed emotional healing. I knew a Christian chiropractor who was building a certain reputation for such healing, so I made an appointment. As I lay on his chiropractic table, he played soft, Christian music in the background and he waved a huge feather, about 3 feet long, over me. He told me to let my emotions go and he would brush them away in the spirit while he recited Scripture. I paid for my session, thanked him for his efforts and left as tied up in knots as I'd been before.

Then I heard about generational curses. As I understood it, somebody in my family's past could have put a curse on me and that's why my life was so twisted. So I went to a weekend retreat that specialized in this kind of praying. I asked the Lord to forgive every ancestor I knew about and everyone I didn't know about. I forgave them as well. I rebuked the curse and commanded it to flee. I could not have told you what any of the curses were because I didn't know. What did they say when they cursed me?

But no, I discovered through this weekend these were their sins which were now being visited upon me, not that they spoke things over their future generations. I know it says in Exodus that God visits the sins of the fathers to the fourth generation, but I read the Bible enough to also know that in Jeremiah and Ezekiel, much later in history than

Moses, God says no longer will the sons pay for the father's sins. Each one will pay for their own. So I left that weekend with no results.

Finally, I turned to the Lord. He was the only One who could help me. I wanted to go back to that happy time I had had with Him in the beginning. I wanted to be in love with Him again and leave the details in His hands. Instead I wallowed in unhappiness. Thoughts, memories, decisions plagued me and my life as a result was chaotic. Only God could help me. I'd tried everything man had to offer.

You might think I tried some pretty dumb things; actually there were more than these. I gave you a sampling. I don't know about you, but when I'm desperate, I'll try anything! I ran to every meeting I could find that talked about inner healing, healing of the emotions, healing of the memories and so on. I knew what it was like to be under grace and I knew I wasn't there anymore.

When I went to the Lord, it was like He opened a door and let fresh air into my soul. He said, "It's not what has happened to you that has hurt you. It's what you believed about yourself because of what happened that has hurt you." He told me I was harboring buried lies that needed to be extracted and replaced with His truth. It's only His Truth that sets us free. He gave me a prayer process to do that. You can find that process in my book *Buried Lies Companion Workbook.*

When I started doing this prayer process I began my trek back to the glory of the grace of God that I longed to return to. I want to live in heaven on earth. I know it's available because I've already lived there.

You have become estranged from Christ, you who attempt to be justified by law; you have fallen from grace (Galatians 5:4).

I knew I had fallen from grace. I knew I had tried by my human efforts to get better. It didn't work. Grace is God-directed, not man-driven. Grace calls for faith and love. The worst part was that I had trampled on the sacrifice of Jesus, claiming it was insufficient to get me set free, to get me clean, to help me over the hurdles in life.

Of how much worse punishment, do you suppose, will he be thought worthy who has trampled the Son of God underfoot, counted the blood of the covenant by which he was sanctified a common thing, and insulted the Spirit of grace? (Hebrews 10:29).

When Jesus was beaten by the Romans, He took on His Body your sicknesses and diseases. That includes the mind and the emotions. You can be sick in both of those just as easily as you can be sick in the body. But Jesus died to heal those. He paid for the maladies (physical, emotional, and mental) of all mankind. Will you insult the Spirit of grace and refuse His gift?

I have a friend whose aunt had been in a mental institution with Alzheimer's for years. She had it to the extent she was violent and had not spoken a recognizable word for the past five years. My friend had the revelation that Jesus had paid for that sickness, so she went to visit her aunt in the institution. An attendant stayed with the aunt day and night to keep her restrained.

My friend told her aunt her revelation about what Jesus had done, that it included mental illness and Alzheimer's is definitely mental illness, a lie of the devil. She told her she knew her aunt could not speak, but she felt sure she could say yes on the inside of her. The aunt got red in the face, looked like she would spring from the bed to assault her niece, so the attendant held her back. But the aunt kept pushing and pushing until the word YES exploded from her mouth. Day by day the aunt got better. It took two weeks for her to become normal again. Glory to God.

Will you keep insulting the Spirit of grace by trying to make things work on your own? By hunting for solutions, even though they seem spiritual, instead of going directly to God your Father? Will you refuse to live in His grace because your friends may not live there? Or even by nursing bad memories and harboring lies?

> *Looking carefully lest anyone fall short of the grace of God; lest any root of bitterness springing up cause trouble, and by this many become defiled; (Hebrews 12:15).*

There are generational lies; there are racial lies; there are territory lies; there are family lies, and more. Read the Bible concerning lies and you'll see how much God hates them. Lies distort His grace. Lies damage you and that breaks God's heart.

He sent His grace, His full favor. Everything He could give you, He already has, and it's all contained in that one word, grace. You obtain it by faith in our Lord Jesus Christ because He did everything necessary for you to receive this grace of God. There is nothing left except for you to live in it.

> *But now the righteousness of God apart from the law is revealed, being witnessed by the Law and the Prophets, (Romans 3:21).*
>
> *Even the righteousness of God, through faith in Jesus Christ, to all and on all who believe. For there is no difference; (V 22).*
>
> *For all have sinned and fall short of the glory of God, (V 23).*
>
> *Being justified freely by His grace through the redemption that is in Christ Jesus, (V 24).*
>
> *Whom God set forth as a propitiation by His blood, through faith, to demonstrate His righteousness, because in His forbearance*

*God had passed over the sins that were
previously committed, (V 25).*

*To demonstrate at the present time His
righteousness, that He might be just and
the justifier of the one who has faith in
Jesus (V 26).*

It was God's full favor that brought Jesus to the earth to
sacrifice Himself for you. He freely justified you, forgave
you, and made you righteous, all by His grace. Because
Jesus was willing to use His blood to buy you back, to
pay for your sins, to be the answer for your injustice, the
response to your iniquities, you are free to live in heaven
on earth. The Father and the Son gave you their full favor,
known as grace.

So now that you know you are the one who put grace
in a shadow, how can you get it back out into the sun?
How can you return to living in the full favor of God?
How can you obtain grace again? There is a way. I'm
calling it Grace Obtained.

Grace Obtained

You must recognize that even though you've been living in darkness for awhile, God has been on the move behind the scenes. He is always bringing you higher in Him. The only reason you have time monitoring your life is because you need time to assimilate the truth of God, to learn who you are in Christ, to understand what He did for you, and to comprehend how you can live fully in His grace, right here, right now.

God exists outside of time. He doesn't need time because He finished the job before He created time. He never starts something if He hasn't already finished it. God, who lives in the Now, created time for you. So be assured that God completed you and your life before the foundations of the earth. You're going to make it. You will become all He created you to be. Right now you are on your journey to that original creation. You are going back to living in grace, God's full favor.

I marvel at the discernment of time that my friends have. Some will tell me they have too much time, the days drag, they hate going to bed, they hate getting up in the morning and their lives seem to progress in slow, slow gear, no matter how hard they work. Others tell me that the more they grow, the faster time goes. Before they know it another year is up. They advance beyond the amount of time they put in. In my opinion, the first example is about people who need more time to arrive at the center of God's grace. The second example is about people who are quickly arriving at a place of full favor and don't need time like they used to.

Let me say it like this. You came from heaven. You were created in the beginning. God wrote a book just about you. Read about that in Psalm 139. Your life was over before you started it. Before the foundations of the earth, you existed and your life had been completely planned. However, God gave you free will.

> *Thus the heavens and the earth, and all the host of them, were finished (Genesis 2:1).*

The host mentioned in this verse is not just the angels in heaven, but the people on the earth. You, as part of the host on earth, were finished before you began. You were born as part of God's heavenly plan. Then when you'd been here awhile, you lost heaven because you followed the first Adam and chose to know sin and evil. Then, you regained heaven by choosing the second Adam, Jesus, as your Lord. He has given you citizenship in heaven again.

> *But we see Jesus, who was made a little lower than the angels, for the suffering of*

death crowned with glory and honor, that He, by the grace of God, might taste death for everyone (Hebrews 2:9).

To the praise of the glory of His grace, by which He made us accepted in the Beloved (Ephesians 1:6).

In Him we have redemption through His blood, the forgiveness of sins, according to the riches of His grace (V 7).

Yes, you'll go to heaven when you die, but you already live there right now, even though you may have no reality about your heavenly abode on earth. When you were first born again, you experienced heaven on earth. Then you lost it by resorting to memories, behaviors and lies. Heaven didn't move; the grace of God didn't leave you; you turned your back on all that favor.

You might argue with me that perhaps it was all part of the Master Plan so that you could then get fixed. How else could you get rid of the memories and lies if grace hadn't gone into shadow?

For years I have given a Buried Lies workshop to help people get rid of the memories and lies. It's been of tremendous help to me as I've unearthed and uprooted over 200 lies in my own life.

But this one thing I know. Having to work out your salvation in this difficult manner is not God's highest and best. Church should not be a hospital where the patients are perpetually getting fixed. Church should be a university where we learn how to be like Jesus. Our job is not to drag ourselves into heaven when we die, grateful that the battle is over. Our job is to stride into heaven just like Jesus, because we so resemble Him.

The Lord gave me this workshop, first for myself and then for others, because I had fallen from His grace, not because I had to go through the pain again. It wasn't in His plan for me or you to backtrack and fall back into old ways from before the new birth.

The divine intention was that within the bloom of your first love with God you would learn your divine position and never fall back. Having fallen, however, you now have to learn how to get back into that desired place. If, initially, you had taken the Word to heart to live it and perform it, to trust it and give it first place in your life, you would not have fallen. You should have weighed the differences. On the one hand the golden life of grace was given to you by God. On the other hand the dismal life of old thoughts and lies was offered by Satan. Well, logically, which one should you have chosen?

Because He is the merciful God that He is, if you choose to walk through the valley of the shadow of death one more time, He'll go with you. He'll prepare a table before you where you can once again choose the glory of grace.

So your question today has to be, 'How do I change so I can live in the full favor of God?' Let me outline it like this:

1. Learn how to get your mind off of yourself and focus on God.

2. Learn how to use the mind of Christ.

3. Learn how to follow the Holy Spirit.

4. Learn how to be the image of Jesus Christ.

1. I don't remember how I learned this one, getting my mind off myself and focusing on Him, but thank God I did. When something is suddenly awry, I'm taken by surprise by something negative, or things simply go wrong, I praise the Lord. I put on an attitude of gratitude. I look for something to be grateful for.

A small example would be what happened just the other day. My new tires cost twice what I expected and I could have panicked because I didn't have enough money in my French bank account to cover it. Immediately, instead of focusing on the lack, I thanked God profusely that I have the money to pay all my bills. I praised and praised and praised and someone put some money in my American account which I withdrew in France through an ATM. The tires are paid for!

Recently a publisher declined to publish one of my novels in French – my current goal. Rather than be upset I chose to thank God profusely for saving me from the wrong publisher. He has just the right one waiting for me at the right moment of time. How do I know that? Because I live in His grace. (Since I wrote the first part of this paragraph I have approached another publisher and he wants all my novels!)

2. I learned to use the mind of Christ when my neighbor and I were in a heated discussion. I don't remember the subject, I only remember knowing I was right and yet I couldn't get him to see my point. Suddenly I stopped. I think I even closed my eyes.

'God, I'm not saying another word until You tell me what to say.' After a few seconds He gave me a sentence to say that resolved the whole discussion. He knows everything. My finite mind knows very little. Let Him tell me the answers. Whatever He tells me to say is always so cordial and kind that even that is enough to resolve conflict.

3. How do you learn to follow the Holy Spirit? It's easy, really. You look for the fruit of the Spirit inside. Start out by looking for peace. The spirit is located around the belly so that's where I look for peace. You may sense the Holy Spirit has something He wants from you, like He may want you to pray and hear the voice of the Lord, so plainly ask Him, "What do You want?"

Other voices will jump in at this point: "Go buy yourself an ice cream cone." "Clean up that mess in the kitchen." "Call your mother." "Sit on the couch till I give you further instruction." I look at each of these and determine which one is carrying peace with it. I have had the Holy Spirit tell me each one of these things at different times, so I have to really LOOK for peace. The fruit of the Spirit cannot be falsified. Satan isn't exactly going to speak with love, joy or peace. He can't. Those fruit belong to the Spirit.

Sometimes I present the Holy Spirit with several choices so that I can follow which way He wants me to go. Again, it will be with that inward witness, just knowing that I know that I know, mainly because of the peace that surrounds the Lord's choice.

4. Becoming the image of Jesus means you spend time in His Presence, observe Him and do what He does. Determine to walk in love at all times because you know God is made of love. Seasoning your talk with the fruit of the Spirit to everyone that God loves – and He loves everyone - makes you resemble Jesus.

Praying in the Spirit is another way to become more like Jesus, but I'm not talking about praying in tongues. I'm talking about all prayer.

> ***Praying always with all prayer and supplication in the Spirit, being watchful to this end with all perseverance and supplication for all the saints- (Ephesians 6:18).***

Did you notice the word 'all'? It means every time you pray your prayer must be in the Spirit. Anything outside of that is praying in the flesh. The word prayer is used 25 times in the Gospels in connection with how the Lord lived His life. Jesus prayed often! When Jesus said 'Follow Me' He meant 'mimic Me'. His is a life of prayer even now.

> *...He always lives to make intercession for them (Hebrews 7:25).*

> *...It is Christ...who is even at the right hand of God, who also makes intercession for us (Romans 8:34).*

If Jesus is praying right now, then it is impossible for you to have fellowship with Him without praying. You cannot become like Jesus unless you, personally, pray in the Spirit. The Holy Spirit is the one who shows you Jesus; He takes you to Him so you can see, observe and become like Him. So if all prayer is to be 'in the Spirit', how do you do that?

> *...constant prayer was offered to God for him by the church (Acts 12:5).*

This Scripture gives you the key to this life of praying in the Spirit. Look closely at the two words 'to God'. The prayer that has power is 'to God'.

You might say, well that's too simple. Yes, it is simple, but we've been blinded by it as well because 'to God' means 'face to face'. You must be there with God when you pray. You must be in His Presence.

This is the powerful key to praying "in the Spirit". You must experience Him to be able to talk to Him. In face to face conversation there is communion. The first key to praying 'in the Spirit' is to wait on the Lord. The church has been taught just to start praying and somewhere along the line the Holy Spirit will join in. However, when you just launch into prayer, all you are doing is speaking empty words. The truth is – you shouldn't say one word until the Holy Spirit moves in your heart. You need to learn to come into the Presence of the Lord and say nothing.

Most people are uncomfortable with silence. They want to talk right away and get everybody to say 'amen' and then they feel they've done their job. But they accomplish nothing that way. Prayer is not just pouring out your heart. You can do that with a psychologist or even with a dog. You want to know God when you pray; you want to comprehend what He wants, what He thinks. Therefore, you have to wait on the Lord.

Wait until the Holy Spirit moves and that's when you know to begin. You know when He manifests. He doesn't sneak up on you. It's quite evident when He shows up. You are to wait until He expresses Himself, even if the waiting drives you mad. How long do you wait? For as long as it takes. If you pray before He shows up, you're wasting your breath and you're wasting your time.

That's the problem with most prayers. People are not willing to wait for the Lord. To help yourself wait you can read the Bible, play a worship tape, or just sit there. As you are waiting, there comes a moment when the heart begins to soften, when the Spirit of God begins to blow, an amazing blanket of love falls, tears may spring forth. Then, and only then, can you ask to see Jesus.

> **Pray without ceasing, (1 Thessalonians 5:17).**

That doesn't mean 24/7. That means praying with such high intention that your prayer is presented until it is answered. Like a hungry baby reaching out for food, he or she cannot be distracted, this is how you must be with your desire to see Jesus. You must reach out to Him until you have Him.

> **Who, in the days of His flesh, when He had offered up prayers and supplications, with vehement cries and tears to Him who was able to save Him from death, and was heard because of His godly fear, (Hebrews 5:7).**

Praying in the Spirit is done with selective words. The prayer is intense with feeling, but you are not blabbing away. You are in agony and ecstasy at the same time. You cannot make this happen in the flesh. In the natural compare this to being very stressed so you jump in the car, go to the beach, or go to the mountains, and walk, or wade, or hike, or just lay in the sun, and the stress goes away.

When you pray in the Spirit it is like that. The peace is glorious. The light warms you. The joy makes you laugh from the inside out. Everything negative disappears. All you want is to be with the Lord. Then all of a sudden you know what to say. It isn't at all what you thought you would say. Your words come out precisely chosen and effective!

> **Likewise the Spirit also helps in our weaknesses. For we do not know what we should pray for as we ought, but the Spirit Himself makes intercession for us with groanings which cannot be uttered. (Romans 8:26).**

When you are reaching out to God with intensity, at that moment the Holy Spirit begins to pray. I wonder how God feels about His children running their own prayer life, ignoring the Holy Spirit and just dominating the airwaves between heaven and earth with what they think. After all, God gave you the Holy Spirit so that He can pray through you. That's the kind of praying all children of God should aspire to achieve, Spirit-led prayer.

In the church there is a mentality of 'going after God' in prayer. But that way of praying is done in the flesh. "Going after God" can be anything from people who beat themselves with whips to people who think making a lot of noise and running around impresses God. It doesn't. The only all night prayer meetings that impress God are the ones that happen because you are in fellowship with Him, time simply goes by and its morning before you know it.

It is so much easier to be in the flesh than to be in the Spirit. You are accustomed to the flesh. You live in the flesh. Being in the Spirit means that when you come into God's presence, you let Him do the work. That's not comfortable. In the flesh it is always you who does the work. But in prayer, He wants to be the one to carry your prayer life. The secret to being like God is to surrender and let God be God, the all-powerful One, in you.

I'm sure you're getting my point by now. To be like Jesus you must be in the Spirit, in His Presence, out of the flesh realm and in His Kingdom. You can have your head in the clouds and your feet on the ground. You can be like Him, in His Presence and still go about your natural, normal occupations. It depends on your focus.

I have a friend who constantly wants to engage my emotions, as if there were a four-alarm fire. She tells me something and wants me to skyrocket, "Oh no! Not that! How can you stand it? You poor thing!" Since that's flesh, I don't do it. Oh, sometimes I get snared but for the most part I stay with Jesus and answer with something that makes her laugh and calm down.

When I first started my trek back into grace I discovered an amazing thing in the Old Testament. Check it out.

> *"This is the word of the LORD to Zerubbabel: 'Not by might, nor by power, but by My Spirit,' Says the LORD of hosts. 'Who are you, O great mountain?*

Before Zerubbabel you shall become a plain! And he shall bring forth the capstone With shouts of "Grace, grace to it!"'" (*Zechariah 4:6-7*).

After the captivity of 70 years in Babylon, some of the people went back to Israel where Shealtiel became governor of Judah. Zerubbabel was his son. The Israelites had yet to finish the building of the temple at the time referred to by this Scripture. Their task was formidable, so what does God say to do about all the obstacles? Shout 'grace, grace' to it!

I thought to myself, *'That's astounding! All I have to do is say "Grace, grace" to something and it will work itself out in my favor? Or even say "Favor, favor" to it?* I started doing that. For example, if I wanted a parking place, as I was driving around hunting for one, I'd say, "Favor, favor to my parking place." Invariably a parking place would open up just in front of the place I wanted to go. That's how grace is. It's right there, wanting to, waiting to take care of everything.

"So now, brethren, I commend you to God and to the word of His grace, which is able to build you up and give you an inheritance among all those who are sanctified (Acts 20:32).

The way I see it, a good parking place is as much a part of my inheritance as living for eternity in heaven. I know that's a hard concept to grasp. How can every little need be filled by grace when I probably don't deserve it. ABSOLUTELY

I DON'T DESERVE IT! God isn't asking that I deserve it. Jesus paid for my lack of ability to deserve it.

He paid for yours, too! Stop trying to work for it and gracefully accept it. You have the full favor of God!

> *Now to him who works, the wages are not counted as grace but as debt (Romans 4:4).*

Grace is what God gives you just because you made Jesus your Lord and you love Him. He wants to lavish you with His bounty, His glory, His ability to provide which is way beyond any ability you can find on earth. The wealthiest man on the earth is not going to make sure you have a good parking place. He doesn't care. But God, the wealthiest being in all the universe, can hardly wait to give you a good parking place. He cares!

> *And God is able to make all grace abound toward you, that you, always having all sufficiency in all things, may have an abundance for every good work (2 Corinthians 9:8).*

Beyond a parking place, God wants all grace working in you for all good things. God wants you to have a sufficiency in all things. I have that now. There isn't anything I can't have or do because of lack in my life. I have all sufficiency in all things. When I want to travel someplace, the money shows up. When I want to publish a book or produce radio stories, the money shows up.

When I want to bless my family or indulge myself, the money shows up.

I have an abundance for every good work. I give monthly support to ten missionaries, two foreign orphans, eleven ministries, plus occasional offerings to other works. I try never to let an offering basket pass me by, you know why? The money always shows up! I hope you give more than I do. I'm just mentioning these things to say, hey! God makes grace abound!

I want it said of me like Paul wrote to the Corinthians about the Macedonians:

> *...who long for you because of the exceeding grace of God in you. Thanks be to God for His indescribable gift! (2 Corinthians 9:14-15).*

I'd like to be known on this earth for the exceeding grace of God in me. It won't be noticed if I don't live smack dab in the middle of that grace and I can't live there if my time and attention are captured by lies and bad memories. Forsaking all that, grace waits for me to plunk myself down in the middle of it, enjoying grace to its limits, of which there are none! Grace is freely given.

My sister asked me one time, "How come God gives you everything you want?" I answered off the top of my head, "I guess it's because I'm His favorite child." Later, in looking at my answer I had to realize that some of God's children are more blessed than others. What puts one in a more favorable position than another? Accepting and receiving His grace, the great gift He gave to Jesus to give to His children. Walking in faith and love, the pillars that put grace into operation.

Peter rebuked Jesus for saying He would be killed and after three days He would rise again. To which Jesus said:

> ... *"Get behind Me, Satan! For you are not mindful of the things of God, but the things of men" (Mark 8:33).*

To paraphrase what Jesus said, "You are not setting your mind on the things of God, but you are setting your mind on the things of man." It is impossible to live smack dab in the grace of God until your mind is set on God.

There's a wonderful old song that goes like this: "I woke up this mornin' with my mind stayed on Jesus. (x 3) Well, Hallelujah! (x 3) I walked around all day with my mind stayed on Jesus. (x3) Well, Hallelujah! (x 3) And when I go to heaven my mind will be stayed on Jesus. (x 3) Well, Hallelujah! (x 3) Therein is the key to grace. Focus on Him and all of heaven focuses on you!

Part two of grace is to find out what He created you to do and then do it. Grace will overwhelm you when you do the job He is waiting for you to do. Look at how Paul expresses this grace on him when he is doing what God wants him to do.

If indeed you have heard of the dispensation of the grace of God which was given to me for you, (Ephesians 3:2).

Of which I became a minister according to the gift of the grace of God given to me by the effective working of His power (Ephesians 3:7).

To me, who am less than the least of all the saints, this grace was given, that I should preach among the Gentiles the unsearchable riches of Christ, (V 8).

You have a destiny, my friend, one selected for you by God and for which He has given you grace. My grace is to write. Every day I ask the Lord what He wants me to do for Him that day and He ALWAYS says, and I mean always, "Write for Me."

One day He said it in this scenario. In prayer I sat still and waited. After about 15 minutes the face of Jesus appeared before me. For the next 30 minutes the Spirit moved me to speak about committing myself to Him. I apologized for my inability to love Him as a husband because of how my 'husbands', my actual husband and my step-father, had treated me. I told Him I wanted to love Him perfectly and asked Him to help me love Him.

I had to keep dragging my wandering mind back to the prayer at hand. Finally, I stayed long enough at the task that

His whole body appeared. It was there all the time but I wasn't focused enough to see it. He took me in His arms and whispered in my ear, "If you love me, write for me."

I've tried things for which I have no grace, like bookkeeping, and it is hideous! When I first started writing short stories for the radio it took me one whole week, ten hours a day, to write one short story of 2000 words. Now it takes me two hours. But in my dozens of years of doing my bookkeeping, the time does not shorten. If anything I think it takes me twice as long to do my administration every month.

> *But to each one of us grace was given according to the measure of Christ's gift (Ephesians 4:7).*
>
> *Therefore, since we are receiving a kingdom which cannot be shaken, let us have grace, by which we may serve God acceptably with reverence and godly fear (Hebrews 12:28).*
>
> *As each one has received a gift, minister it to one another, as good stewards of the manifold grace of God (1 Peter 4:10).*
>
> *Let us therefore come boldly to the throne of grace, that we may obtain mercy and find grace to help in time of need (Hebrews 4:16).*

I don't care what answer is needed grace has it waiting. When I went through my divorce, which is never easy by the way, I cried out before the throne of grace. God never made provision for divorce and therefore He hates it because it is so destructive in His children's lives. I had the judicially-approved divorce papers in my hands and in four weeks time my ticket to France would take me back on the mission field.

Because I had been consumed by divorce proceedings I had inadequately prepared for my departure. My furniture needed to be put into storage and my duplex had to be rented. Four weeks. I sat on my couch and yelled "Help! God, You've got to help me! Help!" at the top of my lungs. In the quiet that followed my outburst, the phone rang.

A man said, "I hear your duplex is for rent." I didn't know what to say. I hadn't mentioned it to anyone. He continued. "My wife and I are out looking at places and we'd like to come by and see it. May I have your address?"

I mumbled, "Okay," gave him my address and hung up the phone. Within ten minutes they were sitting in my living room making small talk.

All of a sudden the man said, "We'll rent your place."

Flabbergasted I said, "Wouldn't you like to see it first?"

He said, "No. I'm sure it's fine." I looked at his wife, surely she would like to see it, but no, she nodded her head in agreement.

I asked, "How did this happen?"

The man looked as calm as a cucumber. "The Lord told us He had a duplex for us to rent and gave us a phone number to call. It was your phone. It was your duplex. If God says its okay, then it's okay with me."

For three weeks I packed and sorted my things without considering I needed to move all my stuff into storage. At church a week before my departure date a young couple visiting from back east sat beside me. They volunteered to move my things into storage. They did it that afternoon. I've never seen them since.

Then I spent the week painting and scrubbing floors and carpet for the couple moving into my place. My ex-husband, the one I had divorced four weeks earlier, volunteered to finish the painting and scrubbing for me. The throne of grace took care of everything.

Since I was totally undone by the divorce, the throne of grace took care of easing me into France as well. Grace is God's full favor: every need met, every provision made, every power, every gift, every authority, everything you can possibly need is yours because of God.

> *Therefore gird up the loins of your mind,*
> *be sober, and rest your hope fully upon the*
> *grace that is to be brought to you at the*
> *revelation of Jesus Christ; (1 Peter 1:13).*

This is not talking about resting your hope on the Day of the Lord when Jesus touches His foot down on the Mount of Olives. This is talking about daily revelation. Jesus wants to reveal Himself to His beloved. The more you hope for that, the more it happens. Apply yourself to the revelation of Jesus and He will reveal Himself and all His glory and all God's grace. It's for you. You might as well abandon yourself to it and get the most out of it you can get. Trust me, I've tried to push the limits and there aren't any!

The Jews have a saying that I really like to quote: "I will do God's will as if it is my will so that He will do my will as if it is His will." Put God first and He'll put you first! God has no limits. Whatever you want, He has it for you and He wrapped it all up in His gift of grace.

Grace is Sufficient

Let's take a look at a Biblical example of grace in order to better understand it. Remember I talked about negative thinking and immersing yourself in old thoughts of defeat and wounding, thereby sending grace into shadow? Now if you think you have it bad, or had it bad, and you can't possibly NOT think about those debilitating, historical things, look at Paul. In his second letter to the Corinthians he lists the conditions of his life.

...in labors more abundant, in stripes above measure, in prisons more frequently, in deaths often (2 Corinthians 11:23b).

From the Jews five times I received forty stripes minus one (V 24).

Three times I was beaten with rods; once I was stoned; three times I was shipwrecked; a night and a day I have been in the deep; (V 25).

In journeys often, in perils of waters, in perils
of robbers, in perils of my own countrymen,
in perils of the Gentiles, in perils in the city,
in perils in the wilderness, in perils in the
sea, in perils among false brethren; (V 26).

In weariness and toil, in sleeplessness often,
in hunger and thirst, in fastings often, in
cold and nakedness- (V 27).

Paul calls all that nothing more than a thorn in his flesh. He asked God for this persecution to be taken away from him. If all that happened to me, I'd be whimpering in the corner like a defeated pup. I would never liken that persecution to being a thorn. In my opinion he experienced torture!

He says he asked God three times to alleviate this suffering, to remove the persecution. Can't you just hear him? 'God!!!!! Keep me safe! Prevent the torture! Guard me! Make the bullies go away! Keep me out of the water! Keep me away from the whips! Fill my belly! Give me comfortable beds to sleep in! After all, I'm working for you! You should be the best boss in the world! You should provide your workers with abundance and security! What's the deal?'

Notice I can write that plea so clearly because it has been one of my own! I know how to cry and complain like the best of them. I've simply learned whimpering, and/or histrionics, doesn't do any good.

Here's God's answer to Paul. It's the same answer He has for you.

> ... *"My grace is sufficient for you, for My strength is made perfect in weakness" (2 Corinthians 12:9a).*

When I read that I was nonplussed to say the least. Sufficient. What a weak word. I don't want something that is just 'sufficient' taking care of me. I don't want to barely get by. I want power. I want authority. I want the odds to overwhelmingly be in my favor. 'Sufficient' doesn't cut it for me.

But the more I contemplated grace, the more I comprehended just how big grace is. The more I realized how God poured everything He has and everything He is into grace and then gave it all to me, the more I realized grace can accomplish absolutely anything. Grace is certainly sufficient to get any job done.

While grace is undertaking to deliver whatever it is you need or even want, there is so much grace that it can never be depleted by the little efforts you require of it.

Surrender. Surrender to His grace. So how do you do that? I mean, practically, in steps you can follow. Paul gives the answer. Admit you are too weak to handle the problem, the persecution, the mountain against you and focus your attention on Him and His attributes. It's that simple.

I like the way the French translate the second part of God's answer: "My grace is enough. My strength manifests itself in weakness." In other words, acknowledging your weakness is the platform on which God's strength will perform.

Paul said he then boasted in his weakness, knowing he couldn't do anything about that thorn in his flesh anyway. But grace could! When you start bragging about God, telling everyone what God is going to do for you or is in the process of doing for you and speaking it out by faith, knowing, believing and triumphing in His victory for you – without figuring it out for yourself or writing down the pros and cons or analyzing just how you can maneuver the situation, GRACE WILL TAKE CARE OF IT.

Now pay attention here. Don't tell God how to do His job! You can't say, 'Now what I want You to do is…' and then explicitly tell Him how you want it done. When I believed God for the million dollars (see my book *Destined for Faith*) I imagined dozens of ways it could come to me. None of those imaginations came to fruition. In fact, the way the Lord chose to bring me the money could never have been conjured up by my imagination!

Let's be honest. Do you really know how to handle your problems? When you wake up each day, can you map the day out and know exactly how it will go? What about your kids? Can you determine their lives for them? Or your grandchildren? You, like everyone else, must answer a resounding NO to all these questions. What you can do in each and every situation is acknowledge your weakness and then thrust the situations into grace. "Grace! Grace!"

Believe God for the result you want and let Him choose the means. I like watching God at work and being totally amazed at the path He chooses. I have two children and five grandchildren. Not one of them is following a path I would have chosen for them. Not one. But it is not my pen that writes their lives in my book. Their lives come from His pen that flows through His book determining each individual destiny according to His purpose and grace. Where will they end up? In heaven with me, having fulfilled their destiny! "Grace! Grace!"

I was 21 years old before I traveled outside the Midwest corridor covering Missouri, Iowa and Minnesota. Never once did I dream of living in France. The Lord surprised me one day by announcing that's where I would go. I was absolutely tongue-tied as a youngster and could not speak in front of a classroom. Now I speak to numbers of audiences, usually to cold gatherings of people I'm meeting for the first time. I don't consider whether I will stutter or stumble; I turn it over to grace before I get there. I have a good time and my audiences seem to enjoy it too. As a child, my authority figures convinced me I was too stupid to be a writer and now that's my main occupation, a task I thoroughly enjoy doing. "Grace! Grace!"

Go ahead! I dare you! Live by the grace of God! You'll make Him very happy that you trust Him enough to live by His grace and that you love Him enough to want to live by His grace. You don't know what to do with yourself anyway, so just do it. Walk on those two pillars of faith and love and be strong in them! Trust Him completely! Trust and obey! Throw doubt out! Love Him thoroughly! Smash sweet superficiality! Live by grace! Be strong in grace! "Grace! Grace!"

ABOUT THE AUTHOR

Marty Delmon comes from a long line of believers. Imprisoned in England for their beliefs, her family came to the New World as Quakers. The other branch came as Methodists. Her great-grandfather, an itinerate minister, wrote in his journal, "The women of my family will publish the Good News of Jesus Christ." Marty is the first to fulfill that prophetic word.

Born in Kansas City, Missouri she claims Minnesota as her state since that's where she spent her high school years. That's also where she developed her love for sports: tobogganing, ice skating, skiing, and swimming. She swam briefly in the Aqua Follies, deterred only by a belligerent toe which cramped the minute it hit the river.

Attending school at Lindenwood College for Women in St. Charles, Missouri, Marty majored in Physical Education and thereafter taught school in San Francisco, California. She married John Pierre Delmon and they produced first a boy, Jeffrey John and then a girl, Jolie Pier.

When the children were ages 7 and 4, Marty's husband confessed his homosexuality. This admission began a long trial of psychologists, counselors, ministers and others who tried to help John overcome his 'condition.' In that epoch everyone believed homosexuals were born that way and there was no help, however, John and Marty plowed on.

During this time of great depression on her part, Jesus surprised Marty by showing up in her life and she became born again. She and her husband attended Rhema Bible Training Center and taking the children, now 18 and 21, they moved to France as missionaries, lasting only three years.

The best thing she did for her husband was to divorce him which made him take responsibility for his 'condition.' He moved into a Christian facility which helps men overcome their sexual deviations. Hence Marty wrote her first book, *Sleeping With Demons*, detailing their path and his subsequent deliverance.

Five weeks after the divorce Marty returned to France as a single missionary. She settled in La Garde Freinet and established a radio ministry where her stories are heard on 107 Francophone stations. She also pioneered a church and taught in a Bible school. Joining International Pentecostal Holiness Church, she returned to the States for three years to raise funds. Back in France she moved to Baillargues outside of Montpellier and focused all her energies on writing. She discontinued public ministry except in the States where she went yearly to raise money.

Out of this intense period of writing, Marty produced 14 books, several stage plays and hundreds of stories for the radio. Her second book, and to date the most successful, is entitled *Buried Lies*, a novel. In her early days of Christianity, in order to lift her out of internal chaos, the Lord gave her a prayer process which plucks the lie out of the soul and plants God's truth instead. As she became freer the Lord asked her to write about the process.

When people read *Buried Lies* they asked Marty to lead workshops. Then they asked her to write a workbook so they could do the process at home. Thus, *Buried Lies Companion Workbook* came into being. Marty also recorded it as an audio book.

Her next novel came out of a certain romance from her youth and is called *Wild Card*. Now she awaits the launching of her current novel *Wild Fire*, a book about The Last Great Revival.

She also has written very effective books describing and explaining the powerful themes in the Bible. She calls them the "Destined" series: *Destined for Healing, Destined for Success, Destined for Love, Destined for Faith, Destined for Grace, Destined for Joy, Destined to Live in the Kingdom.* With more to come.

Marty has recently moved to Neauphle Le Chateau outside of Paris to be closer to her radio studio and the publication of her books. Her son Jeff, his wife Vicky and their two children Alex and Natasha live in Washington, D.C. Her daughter Jolie and her three girls Brittany, Victoria and Madison live in Tulsa, Oklahoma.

THE GREATEST GRACE

I started this book by telling you about my entry into the Kingdom of God through my new birth. There is no other way to enter. Jesus said "I am the Way and the Truth and the Life; no one comes to the Father except through Me." (John 14:6) The door to Heaven is only opened by Jesus Christ and He requires you to become a new 'man' in order to enter, a condition that is achieved through the new birth. I cannot speak for what will happen beyond this life on earth as the Bible only gives very vague hints, but I can adamantly proclaim that the Greatest Grace on earth is the miracle of being born again.

You change. You become the image of God. Greater things come out of you than you ever thought possible. And if you don't, or I should say won't, become born again? If you have not given yourself completely to God Almighty and surrendered to the Lordship of Jesus Christ? Then you have relinquished your eternity to serving the devil in his hell, from which there is no reprieve. And you have missed the mind boggling changes Jesus makes in a new born-again life. The attributes of love, peace and joy change a person immeasurably.

God is not mocked. He knows your heart. You must come to Him for your salvation with a heart that wants to know Him, to love Him, to serve Him and acknowledges that you need a Savior. When He sees your sincerity and your honest desire to become His child and receive the work Jesus did on the cross to retrieve you and make a new covenant with God for you, then the door opens wide and Heaven receives you as one of their own. God your Father adopts you, Jesus your Lord welcomes you and the Holy Spirit of God your guide and companion encompasses you.

I invite you to pray the following Sinner's Prayer and receive the Greatest Grace on the face of this earth, your own new birth into the family of God. May God richly bless you through His Grace! I started this book with my new birth. Let's end it with yours!

THE SINNER'S PRAYER

Jesus, I have sinned against You, Your Father and the Kingdom of God. I've made a mess of things by trying to run my own life and running away from you. Please forgive me. Please apply the blood You so painfully shed to pay for my sins to my spirit, soul and body. I receive You now, Jesus, as my Savior, my Lord, my best Friend, my Master and my Commander in Chief. I will love You, I will serve You, I will honor You, I will proclaim You all the days of my life and I will live with You for eternity in Heaven, the Kingdom of Love. Thank You, Jesus! I am Yours!

Amen.

MORE BOOKS by Marty Delmon

SLEEPING WITH DEMONS
www.tatepublishing.com

Married to a man caught in the trap of sexual deviation, Maggie Dubois takes us on her lone journey through the dark valleys of one-sided marriage. Her passage through the somber alley of longing for love is a story that applies to us all.

Denying the existence of the problem, homosexuality, Maggie is ensnared in the conflict. The climax of the book comes when Maggie breaks through the veil of confusion to recognize the truth and confront the spiritual darkness. Exorcising the evil from her life, Maggie walks free.

"Lessons of Life" could well be a subtitle of this book as Maggie guilelessly shares her insights and revelations of what she discovers as she feels her way through the morass. Her discoveries liberate not only herself but her husband as well. Maggie's victory is everyone's victory: truth and freedom.

BURIED LIES
www.tatepublishing.com

No action evokes as much violent emotion and reaction as does incest. Murder, suicide, hatred, imprisonment, all things ugly in life evolve from this insidious trap set in a female child by her father. Journey with seven women as they confront their past, unearth the lies they have believed about themselves, replacing them with the truth and see the changes made in their lives today. Against all odds, these seven overcame the most heinous of sins: sex forced upon them by Daddy.

Between the ages of 8 and 17 my stepfather perfunctorily raped me. At age 17, I confided in a girl friend and she encouraged me to confront him, asking why he would do such a thing. It never occurred to me I had the personal power to get him to stop, but when I followed her advice, he quit. The trauma stayed with me, however, coloring my future and damaging my potential until I received Jesus as my Lord.

The Holy Spirit led me into a prayer process in which Jesus helped me to uncover the lies I believed about myself because of what happened to me. The important part was that He planted the truth in me to replace those lies. It has made all the difference in my life.

Through the course of interviewing people for the stories I write for radio, I discovered that almost one woman out of two suffered what I suffered in my childhood. I have helped some to unearth the lies and believe the truth, but a book about it will reach far more women than I personally can reach. Therefore I have written Buried Lies.

BURIED LIES COMPANION WORKBOOK

When I came to the Lord I carried a lot of baggage. My illegitimate birth, the continual raping by my stepfather between the ages of 8 and 17, my mother telling me I was too stupid to be a writer so I abandoned my passion, the self-sabotage I committed when I broke up with the love of my life because he was 'too good for me', and then the man I did marry, after ten years of marriage and two children, confessed he was gay.

The Lord gave me a prayer process to clear out the chaos in my life which came not because of all these things that happened to me, but because of the lies I believed about myself because of what happened. I called that book Buried Lies. When people read Buried Lies they asked me to do a workshop to lead them through the prayer process. I thought this to be good as it took me seven hours to complete my first process simply because the prayer is intensely focused and I wasn't accustomed to praying that thoroughly.

Then they asked for a workbook to take home so that they could continue to pull out lies and plant the truth. I decided to put the whole workshop into the workbook, leaving space at the end for them to go through the process themselves and journal about it.

My publisher came up with the best idea when he put the workbook on CD. He even allowed me to do the recording. Now people can take the workshop anywhere they want and the final of the four CDs leads the listener through the prayer process. There is one more prayer to go through which the Lord also gave me for the purpose of hearing Him more clearly. I call it 'The Garden'.

WILD CARD
www.tatepublishing.com

His dream.... Ron La Fave had charted his path and meticulously pursued it. Deflecting every distraction and breaking his own heart in the process, he persevered to the point of wounding his loved ones as he doggedly attained the success that powered his dreams.

But, Ron failed to recognize the reality of evil. Dreams can be sabotaged from within, yet the threat from without comes like a sidewinder. One strike, one puncture and the aspiration deflates like a party balloon flailing wildly about the room.

Wherever he turned, the serpent hoisted its evil head. His Board of Directors threw him out; his wife left; his mentor disowned him; his bank accounts closed; his reputation tanked and the industry blackballed him. Left with nothing, he retreated to Jackson Hole.

Counting on the mountains to restore him, he hid in the Tetons. However, a certain Presence wouldn't leave. Ron found himself grappling with distractions he could not deflect and instead of the peace he sought, he tormentedly confronted good and evil.

Learning to accept the one and reject the other, a spiritual path opened which revealed success beyond his wildest dreams. Suddenly, every conflict in life resolved itself.

WILDFIRE
www.tatepublishing.com

What do Dempsey Davenport, a professional golfer, Bart Connors, a range riding cowboy and Jazz Zimmerman, an abandoned woman have in common? Absolutely nothing, nevertheless they kindle the fire of The Last Great Revival. Unaware, they plow through demons and receive angelic help.

Dempsey loses his career but rallies to pioneer a Christian coffee house. Pastor Bart's church supports outreaches to heal society's ills but Bart himself only overcomes death through the prayers of multitudes. Jazz uses an unconventional therapy to set drug addicts free but the State closes the facilities. Yet something greater arises, something that changes the world.

As these ordinary people demonstrate, whether or not you are aware of the forces of Good and Evil, they are aware of you. An eternal war wages where you are the prize. Satan wants to stop you in order to thwart The Last Great Revival.

Join author Marty Delmon on a quick-paced spiritual thrill ride that captures a true picture of the battle lines between success and defeat, and shows that revival can truly spread like Wild Fire.

DESTINED FOR SUCCESS
www.rpjandco.com

Isaiah foretold the cross, the price Jesus would pay and the benefits we would receive. He mentioned prosperity. "The chastisement of our prosperity was upon Him," Is 53:5. The Hebrew word is SHALOM! While the translators used the word 'peace' in this verse, both prosperity and peace are the meanings of SHALOM. The two words are interchangeable. Can you have peace without prosperity? Doesn't prosperity bring peace? Jesus paid for you to have prosperity. It's a new-birth right. **Destined for Success** defines that prosperity and directs you to the path to receive it. SHALOM!

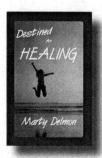

DESTINED FOR HEALING
www.rpjandco.com

All around the author sees unnecessary sickness and pain. She sees people trying to explain away their failure at being healed. The author knows from personal experience the triumph of overcoming the disease of the body and wanted to share the knowledge she's gained. May the Body of Christ truly be transformed by accepting the healing that Jesus bought for us with His body.

DESTINED FOR LOVE
www.rpjandco.com

Love is a force. Without a doubt it is the strongest force on the earth. For example, faith works by love and we know that we cannot please God without faith, hence, without love there can be no faith and without faith there is no pleasing God. In **Destined for Love**, Author Marty Delmon takes us on a journey through the Bible to demonstrate what love is, how to use it and what amazing results are intrinsically woven into the practice of love.

Jesus gave the Body of Christ one command: those who live in the Kingdom of God would be known by those who do not as Christians. How would the unsaved know that certain ones are Christians? By our love for others living in the Kingdom. Not by our love for the world. The world abuses the gifts given to them, but when they see how much we Christians love each other a certain hunger is created. How much love for one another do we actually see in our churches? Are we making the unsaved jealous yet?

Christians are DESTINED FOR LOVE. The question is, will we fulfill our destiny? Will we find the source of all good things coming down from the Father of Lights? It is essential to understand love because the promises of God are all based on love. In all honesty we have to answer the question that asks if we have been having trouble receiving what we need and want from God. Maybe the answer can be found in how much love we are giving.

DESTINED FOR FAITH
www.rpjandco.com

What is it that makes a Christian's life different from that of a person who doesn't believe in Jesus Christ the Son of God? Gosh, where to begin? There can be a long list, but it really boils down to one thing. We trust God.

The major benefit of having faith is huge! Something dynamic comes from God our Father and that power delivers to us what we believe for God to provide. It is by faith that we draw what we want into our natural, physical life. God doesn't just want us to have "pie in the sky in the sweet by and by!" He wants us to have "steak on our plate while we wait!" Only faith can bring that pie out of the sky and make it become steak on our plate. This takes a profound level of trust that is not for the lukewarm. It's an all or nothing faith. Sure we can do it. It's just a matter of answering this question: do we want it bad enough?"

This book will instruct the reader in how to turn life into an adventure of faith, the kind of faith that moves God. The Bible says it's faith that pleases Him. The Lord wants to change our world through our faith. That's what makes Him happy.

About the Publisher

In 2004, the Spirit of God birthed RPJ & Company according to Romans 14:17.

RPJ & Company, Inc. began publishing Christian books for pastors, leaders, ministers, missionaries, and others with a message to help the Body of Christ. Our published books continue to empower, inspire and motivate people to aspire to a higher level of understanding through the written word.

Our company is dedicated to assisting those individuals who desire to publish Christian books that are uplifting, inspiring and self-help in nature. We also offer assistance for those who would like to self-publish.

The special service that we provide is customized, quality layout and design for every client. This gives every new author a chance at becoming successfully-published. For every book, we offer exposure and a worldwide presence to help the book and the author become discovered!

"As an author and publisher, I can guide you through the steps of creating, editing, proofreading and providing you with a professional layout and design for any printed item, one you'll be proud to call your own."

- Kathleen Schubitz
Founder and CEO

RPJ & COMPANY, INC.
"Where quality and excellence meet face to face!"

 www.store.rpjandco.com

Lightning Source UK Ltd.
Milton Keynes UK
UKOW030639100412

190407UK00001B/1/P